Ten Poe
about Tr.....

OUTBOUND

Candlestick Press

Published by:
Candlestick Press,
Diversity House, 72 Nottingham Road, Arnold, Nottingham NG5 6LF
www.candlestickpress.co.uk

Design and typesetting by Craig Twigg

Printed by Bayliss Printing Company Ltd of Worksop, UK

Selection and Introduction © André Naffis-Sahely, 2023

Cover illustration © Gail Brodholt
https://gailbrodholt.com/

Candlestick Press monogram © Barbara Shaw, 2008

© Candlestick Press, 2023

ISBN 978 1 913627 25 6

Acknowledgements

The poems in this pamphlet are reprinted from the following books, all by
permission of the publishers listed unless stated otherwise. Every effort has been
made to trace the copyright holders of the poems published in this book. The
editor and publisher apologise if any material has been included without
permission, or without the appropriate acknowledgement, and would be glad to
be told of anyone who has not been consulted.

Thanks are due to all the copyright holders cited below for their kind permission.

Mahmoud Darwish, *Unfortunately, It Was Paradise*, trans. Munir Akash and
Carolyn Forché (University of California Press, 2003) by permission of the
Copyright Clearance Center. Paul Durcan, *Snail in my Prime: Selected Poems*
(Vintage Publishing, 1999) by permission of David Higham Associates. Langston
Hughes, *The Collected Poems of Langston Hughes* (Vintage Books, 1995) by
permission of David Higham Associates. Ada Limón, *The Carrying*
(Minneapolis: Milkweed Editions, 2018) by kind permission of BOA
Permissions. Declan Ryan, *Poetry Ireland Review Issue 118* (April 2016) - The
Rising Generation Issue - ed. Vona Groarke, by kind permission of the author.
André Naffis-Sahely, poem first appeared in this pamphlet. Mary Ruefle,
Apparition Hill (CavanKerry Press, 2002) by kind permission of BOA
Permissions. Judith Wright, *A Human Pattern: Selected Poems* (Carcanet Press,
2010).

All permissions cleared courtesy of Dr Suzanne Fairless-Aitken
c/o Swift Permissions swiftpermissions@gmail.com

Where poets are no longer living, their dates are given.

Contents

Introduction

In October 1844, Wordsworth wrote to the Prime Minister William Gladstone to protest the planned extension of the railway into the heart of the Lake District in the north of England, enclosing a poem he'd specially penned for the occasion. "Is then no nook of English ground secure / From rash assault?" he asks, in the opening lines of 'On the Projected Kendal and Windermere Railway', comparing the engineering works to a military invasion, and the laying of tracks to a "blight", encouraging his readers to raise their voices against this "wrong". Not in my backyard, Wordsworth entreats! Nevertheless, not wishing to be seen as a reactionary, set against all forms of progress, he soon directed his loyal followers to an earlier sonnet he'd written, namely 'Steamboats, Viaducts, and Railways', in which, while nonetheless lamenting the fact that railways, alongside steamboats and viaducts, "mar / the loveliness of nature", he also wagered that Time, being pleased with humanity's "triumphs o'er his brother Space", would greet this revolutionary method of transportation "with cheer sublime".

Edna St. Vincent Millay's poem 'Travel', where she exclaims, "there isn't a train I wouldn't take, / No matter where it's going" is imbued with the febrile excitement prompted by this new mode of transportation, as is Mary Ruefle's 'Timberland', where she hitches a free ride "in the boxcar of a freight train". Trains also stir ruminations of the heart, like in Declan Ryan's 'A Valley of Applause', and Paul Durcan's poem about a love affair aboard the 'Red Arrow' in Russia. Not that this new mode of transportation was immediately available to all, as Alice Duer Miller reminds us in 'Why We Oppose Women Travelling in Railway Trains'.

Admittedly, trains are not quite as cutting edge as they were in Wordsworth's time, but freight still rolls, railroad planning still shapes our cities and the vocabulary of the railways still permeates our speech. We call disasters a train wreck, get distracted by a train of thought, dream of boarding the gravy train, get derailed, or find ourselves on the wrong side of the tracks. Who knows how long trains will endure before we trundle them off to a museum? There's a ballad by the American labour troubadour Utah Phillips – too long to include in these pages – whose refrain goes: "Daddy, What's a train? Is it something I can ride? / Does it carry lots of grown up folks and little kids inside / Is it bigger than our house? - oh, how can I explain / When my little boy asks me, 'Daddy, what's a train?'" Let's hope nobody ever gets asked that question.

André Naffis-Sahely

Travel

The railroad track is miles away,
   And the day is loud with voices speaking,
Yet there isn't a train goes by all day
   But I hear its whistle shrieking.

All night there isn't a train goes by,
   Though the night is still for sleep and dreaming,
But I see its cinders red on the sky,
   And hear its engine steaming.

My heart is warm with the friends I make,
   And better friends I'll not be knowing;
Yet there isn't a train I wouldn't take,
   No matter where it's going.

Edna St. Vincent Millay (1892 – 1950)

A Valley of Applause

Is this where we would have had to go?
We might have made it here –
the other side of a bridge
from everyone we loved,
our plans, the shape we'd made
in the universe's lack.

Just off a train,
the rails curling round
and out of sight
we could, your hand in mine,
have stood a state of willed amnesia –
the sky a pyre – shaken off our shame
like dogs who'd swum through oil.

Frontier life,
water and shelter life,
imagine our first night:
unstoried earth to walk on,
a river to wash our hands
and mouths with,
hills to stop our gods from staring in.

The only words we'd need
would be 'I'm safe'
or 'start again',
your scent a lotus flower,
my skin broken by your teeth
like soft applause.

Remember you said
we should admit the way we felt
however difficult?
I'm saying now,
too late for you to waste your life.
Here isn't where we would have gone

but where I always was:
cut off from sun,
green-shadowed on all sides by noble boundaries.
The sky is hellfire.
I burn like coal,
whose heart is unforgetful coal.

Declan Ryan

A seat on a train

Scarves that don't belong to us. Lovers at the last minute. The light of the
station. Roses that deceive a heart in search of tenderness. Treacherous tears
on the platform. Myths that don't belong to us. They traveled from *here*. Do
we have a certain *there*, so that we might rejoice when we arrive? Tulips are
not for us, so why should we love the railway? We travel in search of nothing,
but we don't like trains when new stations are new places of exile. Lanterns,
but not for us, to see our love waiting in the smoke. An express train to cross
the lakes. In every pocket, keys to a house and a family photograph. All the
passengers return to their families, but we do not return to any home.
We travel in search of nothing, so that we may achieve the rightness of
butterflies. Windows, but not for us, to exchange greetings in every language.
Was the earth any clearer when we rode the horses of the past? Where are
these horses? Where are the maidens of the songs? And when in us are the
songs of nature? I am distant even from my own distance. How distant, then,
is Love? Fast girls, like robbers, hunt us. We forget addresses scrawled on
train windows. We, who fall in love for ten minutes, cannot enter a house
twice. We cannot become an echo twice.

Mahmoud Darwish (1941 – 2008)
Translated from Arabic by Munir Akash and Carolyn Forché

The Trains

Tunnelling through the night, the trains pass
in a splendour of power, with a sound like thunder
shaking the orchards, waking
the young from a dream, scattering like glass
the old men's sleep, laying
a black trail over the still bloom of the orchards;
the trains go north with guns.

Strange primitive piece of flesh, the heart laid quiet
hearing their cry pierce through its thin-walled cave
recalls the forgotten tiger,
and leaps awake in its old panic riot;
and how shall mind be sober,
since blood's red thread still binds us fast in history?
Tiger, you walk through all our past and future,
troubling the children's sleep; laying
a reeking trail across our dream of orchards.

Racing on iron errands, the trains go by,
and over the white acres of our orchards
hurl their wild summoning cry, their animal cry…
the trains go north with guns.

Judith Wright (1915 – 2000)

Timberland

Paul's Fish Fry in Bennington, Vermont, is no longer
Closed For The Season Reason Freezin. The umbrellas
have opened over the picnic tables and the bees are
beginning to annoy the french fries, the thick shakes
and real malts of my past:

I am thirteen thousand miles removed, on the delta
of the Pearl River, eating a litchi. Its translucent flesh just
burst in my mouth; shreds of it glitter between my teeth.
I smile but the fruit seller is sour. In fact, he is so sour
the only man on earth he resembles is Paul. But the litchi...

Actually none of this has happened yet. I am nineteen
years old. I am riding in the boxcar of a freight train
hurtling toward Pocatello, Idaho. In a very dangerous move
I maneuver my way back to the car behind me, an open gondola
carrying two tons of timberland eastward out of Oregon:

it is here I will lie all night, my head against the logs,
watching the stars. No one knows where I am. My mother thinks
I am asleep in my bed. My friends, having heard of a derailment
at ninety miles an hour on the eastbound freight, think I am
dead. But I'm *here*, hurtling across the continent with un-

believable speed. We are red-hot and we go, the steel track
with its imperceptible bounce allows us to go, our circuitous
silhouette against the great Blue Mountains and my head in a
thrill watching the stars: I am not yet at a point in my life
where I am able to name them, but there are so many and they are

so white! I'm hurtling toward work at Paul's, toward the litchi-
bite in Guangzhou, toward the day of my death all right, but all
I can say is I am *happyhappyhappy* to be here with the stars and
the logs, with my head thrown back and then pitched forward
in tears. And the litchi! it's like swallowing a pearl.

Mary Ruefle

Cargo

I wish I could write to you from underwater,
       the warm bath covering my ears—
one of which has three marks in the exact
shape of a triangle, my own atmosphere's asterism.

Last night, the fire engine sirens were so loud
they drowned out even the constant bluster
       of the inbound freight trains. Did I tell you,
the R. J. Corman Railroad runs 500 feet from us?

Before everything shifted and I aged into this body,
  my grandparents lived above San Timoteo Canyon
where the Southern Pacific Railroad roared each scorching
California summer day. I'd watch for the trains,
howling as they came.

Manuel is in Chicago today, and we've both admitted
     that we're travelling with our passports now.
Reports of ICE raids and both of our bloods
are requiring new medication.

I wish we could go back to the windy dock,
drinking pink wine and talking smack.
Now, it's gray and pitchfork.

The supermarket here is full of grass seed like spring
       might actually come, but I don't know. And you?

I heard from a friend that you're still working on saving
    words. All I've been working on is napping, and maybe
being kinder to others, to myself.

Just this morning, I saw seven cardinals brash and bold
       as sin in a leafless tree. I let them be for a long while before
I shook the air and screwed it all up just by being alive too.

Am I braver than those birds?

Do you ever wonder what the trains carry? Aluminum ingots,
              plastic, brick, corn syrup, limestone, fury, alcohol, joy.

All the world is moving, even sand from one shore to another
is being shuttled. I live my life half afraid, and half shouting
at the trains when they thunder by. This letter to you is both.

Ada Limón

The Red Arrow

In the history of transport – is there any other history? –
The highest form of transport is the Red Arrow,
The night train from Leningrad to Moscow.
With whom will I be sharing my compartment tonight?
The editor of the *Jazz Front Gazette*, it transpires.
But, affable, polite, as she is, how can she compare
With Svetka with whom I shared in 1981?
We sat up half the night chin-wagging, colloguing,
And when awkwardly I began to undress and she said:
"Ah yes, it is alright – would you like to?"
Naturally I liked to,
And the train was about half way between Leningrad and Moscow
When I fell out of her bunk on to the floor
And the wagon-lady put her head in the door
To check what was the matter
And Svetka said in Russian: "These foreigners
They cannot even keep from falling out of bed –
Always needing to be treated like babies."
The wagon-lady grunted and slid the door shut
And I climbed back into the bunk with Svetka.
Each time we made love she groaned:
"I am the little horse in your snow."
I let up the window blind and, as we made love again –
A blizzard upside down at the windowpane –
When she opened her eyes, she murmured
"You are snowing on my tail, my dear man."
As the Red Arrow flew into Moscow, Svetka said:
"My dear man, you must meet me tomorrow.
Tell them you have a problem with your business.
Meet me in the Melodiya Music Store on Kalinin.
I will be in the Classical Russian Music section.
Look me up under Rachmaninov."

It was a grey Moscow afternoon – not a bead of sunlight –
But we traipsed up and down the Arbat in seventh heaven.
"My dear, dear man," she keeps murmuring over and over.
Although that was all of seven years ago –
She who shot the Red Arrow through my heart.

Paul Durcan

Why We Oppose Women Travelling in Railway Trains

1. Because travelling in trains is not a natural right.
2. Because our great-grandmothers never asked to travel in trains.
3. Because woman's place is the home, not the train.
4. Because it is unnecessary; there is no point reached by a train that cannot be reached on foot.
5. Because it will double the work of conductors, engineers and brakemen who are already overburdened.
6. Because men smoke and play cards in trains. Is there any reason to believe that women will behave better?

Alice Duer Miller (1874 – 1942)

The Skunk Train

What if the story had ended there, when the aptly-named narco boat,
the *Frolic*, its V-shaped belly sliced open by reefs, spilled its treasures
into the mussel-grey ocean? Nobody would ever smoke the opium
the ship had carried, but the white china cups destined for San Francisco

survived, cracked by rocks into something resembling seashells,
and given a second life by the clay-loving Pomo, before they too
were driven away. It needn't have gone any further; the price
of dope might have risen, more blood might have been spilled

down the city's hills, but the coast of Mendocino could have
remained untouched, just a little longer. How much history
can reside in the hands of chancers, like the shit-heels, who,
intent on pillaging the *Frolic's* lost cargo, on reaching that

distant shore, gazed at the world's tallest forest rising above
the bluffs, and saw – nothing but money. A sad mist envelops
Noyo Harbor, where the schooners once anchored, waiting
for their hauls of timber, but little remains of the lumber yard

on Main Street, the partially crumbled walls bleached like
a whale's carcass. A frail old woman waves a sign
that reads STOP THE STINK, meaning the Skunk Train's
smelly, smoky siren song as it chugs down the hills laden

with day-trippers, the last iron horse of the redwoods.
The single Eagle left in town, votes to dissolve the lodge,
and turns off the lights. Later that night when the moon rises,
I watch the hunt for abalone begin, lose myself in the angry

roar and wonder: if the ocean begot us, what future hunter
hides beneath those frothy waves, gestating in sea-slime,
evolving, biding its time? The old-timey conductor yells
all aboard!, and all I want to do is jump off. Maybe I will.

André Naffis-Sahely

One-Way Ticket

I pick up my life
And take it with me
And I put it down in
Chicago, Detroit,
Buffalo, Scranton,
Any place that is
North and East –
And not Dixie.

I pick up my life
And take it on the train
To Los Angeles, Bakersfield,
Seattle, Oakland, Salt Lake,
Any place that is
North and West –
And not South.

I am fed up
With Jim Crow laws,
People who are cruel
And afraid,
Who lynch and run,
Who are scared of me
And me of them.

I pick up my life
And take it away
On a one-way ticket –
Gone up North,
Gone out West,
Gone!

Langston Hughes (1901 – 1967)